MIMI PINSON

Borgo Press Books by FRANK J. MORLOCK

Castor and Pollux and Other Opera Libretti (Editor)
The Chevalier d'Éon and Other Short Farces (Editor)
Chuzzlewit
Congreve's Comedy of Manners
Crime and Punishment
Cyrano and Molière: Five Plays by or About Molière (Editor)
Doctor Scratch and Other Plays (Editor)
Falstaff (with Shakespeare, John Dennis, & William Kendrick)
Fathers and Sons
Herculaneum & Sardanapalus: Two Opera Libretti (Editor)
The Idiot
Isle of Slaves and Other Plays (Editor)
Jurgen
Justine
The Key to the Great Gate and Other Plays
The Londoners & The Green Carnation: Two Plays
Lord Jim
The Madwoman of Beresina & Other Napoleonic Plays (Editor)
Mimi Pinson and Other Plays (Editor)
Notes from the Underground
Oblomov
Old Creole Days
Outrageous Women: Lady Macbeth and Other Plays (Editor)
Peter and Alexis
The Princess Casamassima
A Raw Youth
Salammbô & Dido: Two Operas (Editor)
The Stendhal Hamlet Scenarios and Other Shakespearean Shorts from the French (Editor)
Two Voltairean Plays: The Triumvirate; Comedy at Ferney
Whitewashing Julia and Other Plays
The Widow's Husband; and, Porthos in Search of an Outfit: Two Dumasian Comedies (Editor)
A Yiddish Hamlet and Other Plays
Zeneida & The Follies of Love & The Cat Who Changed into a Woman: Two Plays (Editor)

MIMI PINSON AND OTHER PLAYS

FRANK J. MORLOCK,

EDITOR

THE BORGO PRESS
MMXIII

MIMI PINSON AND OTHER PLAYS
Copyright © 2001, 2003, 2005, 2006, 2013 by Frank J. Morlock
FIRST EDITION

Published by Wildside Press LLC

www.wildsidebooks.com

DEDICATION

For My Daughter, Michelle

CONTENTS

MIMI PINSON, by Jean Bayard and Philippe
    Dumanoir 9
CAST OF CHARACTERS. 10
THE PLAY 11
THE TYPE YOU DON'T MARRY, by Édouard
    Pailleron 129
CAST OF CHARACTERS. 130
THE PLAY 131
MARRIED SINCE NOON, by William Busnach
    and Armand Liorat 163
CAST OF CHARACTERS. 164
THE PLAY 165
ABOUT THE AUTHOR 189

MIMI PINSON

A VAUDEVILLE IN ONE ACT
BY JEAN BAYARD AND
PHILIPPE DUMANOIR

CAST OF CHARACTERS

MIMI PINSON, working girl

PAUL, her neighbor

SERAPHIN, also her neighbor

ESTRAGON, porter

THE PLAY

The stage represents Mimi's room on the fifth floor. An entrance door at the back, slightly to the left, opening on the landing; to the right, nearer the audience, a door blocked off, beside which is placed a chest of drawers; to the left, a chimney. A window closer to the audience by which is a cage containing two canaries; an alcove at the back; to the right of the door a small table on which is a doll's head; to the left another table slightly bigger.

AT RISE, Mimi comes out of the alcove, finishes dressing, and runs to the window which she opens.

MIMI

Ah! My God!—the sun is already on the neighboring chimney! My cheap clock is striking six o'clock and I am not yet at work! Quick! quick! (she sits at the table at the right and takes a bonnet to which she adds flowers)

(singing)

How not to

Set to work

Gaily in the morning!

When a song gives us courage

And work is an amusement!

This little bonnet,

New and chic,

Is going to the carnival

Dancing

Since pleasure awaits her.

I must make her while singing.

How not to, etc.

SERAPHIN

(half opening the door at the back)

There she is!— Let's slip in. (he enters, and gently shuts the door; he holds a bouquet and carries papers under his arm) Mamzelle Mimi! (aside) She doesn't see me! This happens to her every time she turns her back to me. (placing his hand on his heart, and blowing her extravagant kisses) My! My! My!

MIMI

Huh? (turning) Ah! It's you, my neighbor. What is it you are doing like that? (she copies his gestures)

SERAPHIN

Me? I—I was practicing gestures of hypnosis.

MIMI

Really!—they resembled gestures of telegraphy.

SERAPHIN

There is some resemblance. (presenting his bouquet) My neighbor.

MIMI (coyly)

For goodness sake! A bouquet, for me—Mimi Pinson, couturier!

SERAPHIN

Doggone! It seems like they go together!

MIMI

Say, do you take me for a great lady or a dancer, eh? A pot of flowers, I don't say, but a bouquet! (taking it) Thanks, indeed, neighbor.

SERAPHIN

Right! This is a gallantry practiced in the highest society. (tittering) And as we both lodge on the fifth floor—

MIMI

That's our floor— Ah! The pretty rose! Neighbor, it would be really sweet of you, if—

SERAPHIN

If what? If what?

MIMI

If you would put some water in my beautiful cup— Over there—on the chimney.

SERAPHIN (eagerly)

Right away, Mamzelle Mimi— For you nothing is too costly for me—! —Nothing!

MIMI

Oh! That won't ruin you— Bring it over here—to my work table—in front of me. (She puts the bouquet in the glass) There—that way I won't be alone. (she places the vase on the table in front of her)

SERAPHIN

What! Not alone? And me! And me! Am I not worth a rose?

MIMI

Oh, you—Mr. Seraphin—here it is a month that you've been installed in the room opposite—that we've been neighbors on the landing, door to door, nose to nose—and still, all I know is your name—which is very beautiful.

SERAPHIN (modestly)

It is worthy—Seraphin—there's something heavenly in it.

MIMI

Especially under the eaves— But information stops there—and one wants to know who one is receiving— What is your situation, then?

SERAPHIN

Yes, wait! (aloud) Mademoiselle Mimi!

MIMI

Mr. Seraphin!

SERAPHIN

Haven't you told me often that you have a very particular horror of bailiffs?

MIMI

Oh God, process servers!—and the proprietors! I abominate them! Only the proprietors, I abominate them only every three months, around the eighth—while the process servers, it's all year long.

SERAPHIN

It's chronic.

MIMI

Not that I'm afraid of them—I've never been seized.

SERAPHIN

Too bad! (Mimi is startled) I mean—too bad for them! But why?

MIMI

It's an idea that I have.

SERAPHIN

Well, since you want to know my profession—I reveal it to you (assuming a grave tone)—that I am not a process server's clerk. (aside) What cunning!

MIMI (rising)

Heavens—that reply! I know quite well you are not a minister, either— But I want to know.

SERAPHIN

Well, I am going to tell you everything.

MIMI (cleaning up the table on the right)

Ah!

SERAPHIN

My situation—my profession—my social position— Oh, my Mimi! It's to love you like a madman! (aside) This is cowardice!

MIMI

To love me?

SERAPHIN (aside)

At the very least she's going to scratch my eyes out.

MIMI (gaily)

This great secret!— That cannot be all?

SERAPHIN

Huh?

MIMI

From the moment you came to lodge on my floor— Everybody who's lived here for the last three years— haven't they loved me like madmen? One after the other? It's agreed, it's accepted in the house—absolutely like the sou to the pound and the log to the janitor—they wouldn't have rented to you without it.

SERAPHIN (Uneasily)

And you?

MIMI (proudly)

Oh! Me! (changing tone) Ask news of me in the neighborhood.

SERAPHIN (with passion)

Well! Yes, I believe you—I believe the neighborhood— Besides, do I have need to inform myself? Ah God! (aside) It's over already. (aloud) Yes, you are a virtuous couturier—an incomparable couturier—and I award you my heart as the prize of your virtue! I will speak—I will shout from the rooftops—

MIMI (laughing)

You are well situated for that.

SERAPHIN

I shall proclaim that no other man—(rapping is heard on the blocked door) What's that?

PAUL (outside)

Neighbor!

MIMI

What, neighbor?

PAUL

Hello.

MIMI

Hello.

SERAPHIN (uncomfortable)

Where's this anonymous "Hello" coming from?

PAUL

Can I come in, neighbor?

MIMI

Anytime, neighbor.

SERAPHIN

Another one.

MIMI

One quite new—by the month—Mr. Paul—Don't you know him?

SERAPHIN

Paul? Wait! Why yes, I knew one— No, his name was Adrien.

MIMI

Ah! This one's named Paul only.

SERAPHIN

And he lives?

MIMI

In the room on the side.

SERAPHIN

Does he often tap on your partition?

MIMI

No, at the door.

SERAPHIN

Here?

MIMI

This one here—which is blocked off.

SERAPHIN (suspiciously)

Completely blocked?

MIMI

In perpetuity! If ever it opens, I permit you to think whatever you like.

SERAPHIN

Oh! I—(rapping at the door at the back) What is it now?

PAUL

My neighbor.

MIMI

Always the same—Come in, neighbor!

(Paul enters with some bread and cherries.)

PAUL

Ah, pardon, neighbor—you have company.

MIMI

No, no— Come in— This gentleman is not company.

SERAPHIN

What do you mean, I'm not? (aside) Ah! Dammit! He's a good-looking man, the other neighbor!

MIMI (taking Paul by the hand)

Pardon—as in society. (presenting him to Seraphin) Mr. Paul, commission merchant—on leave.

SERAPHIN (bowing his head)

Ah! I am deeply honored.

MIMI

Mr. Seraphin—not the clerk of a process server.

PAUL

Ah! (imitating Seraphin) I am truly honored. (gaily) My neighbor, I am coming to lunch with you. (he places his cherries on the chest of drawers)

SERAPHIN (aside)

For goodness sake—don't be shy!

MIMI

Heavens! It's just my hour—and that of my canaries—It must be yours, Mr. Seraphin.

PAUL (laughing)

Ah! Ah! Ah!

SERAPHIN (stung)

What is the object of your thought?

PAUL

My neighbor—would you like to share my cherries?

MIMI (busy)

No, no thanks—I am going to light the furnace to warm my milk.

SERAPHIN (following her)

What is the object of—

MIMI

You are boring me! Rather, give me a slip of paper.

PAUL (eagerly)

Here, neighbor, here. (he tears a letter)

MIMI

Thanks, neighbor.

SERAPHIN

(looking at him scornfully)

Vapid gallantry! He pays her homage on the back of a letter!

PAUL (aside)

I already said that I will never see her again.

MIMI

(rolling the paper as she lights it and reading it, indifferently)

To Baron de—

PAUL (running to get the paper back)

Give me that, neighbor! I won't allow you to take the trouble. (he lights the paper, aside) Clumsy that I am!

MIMI

What's that signify? The Baron de—?

PAUL (negligently)

I don't know—it's a paper that I got from there. (he points to those Seraphin has placed on the table)

SERAPHIN

There! Ah! Why—don't burn my dossiers, hey!

MIMI

Your—

SERAPHIN

I mean—the dossier of one of my friends who confided it to me. (strutting) A notary's clerk. (aside) Goose that I am!

MIMI

(to Paul who is lighting the fire)

That's it—take my place, while I go down to get my small loaf of bread.

SERAPHIN (offering his arm)

Ah! Neighbor, you will allow me—

MIMI

Not at all—you are going to have your job, too—you are going to give lunch to my canaries.

SERAPHIN

Huh?

MIMI

(going to get the cage, which she delivers to Seraphin) And pay careful attention to it—one of them only drinks when you hold him—I raised him like that. (she puts the bird in his hand)

SERAPHIN (aside)

What a deplorable education! (aloud) Ah, indeed, but—

MIMI

Make him drink.

SERAPHIN (twisting the cage)

Which side? (they laugh) It's because they are very embarrassing, these animals.

MIMI

Pity yourself then. (pointing to Paul, who is fixing the oven) The most embarrassed is the one who is tending to that—

PAUL

There!

SERAPHIN

You said it.

MIMI

And then with me, it's like this. (sings)

It's Mimi the grisette.

Poor little girl

In her room

She's got no maid

Therefore the neighbors

Have to share

The housekeeping chores

And all the little tasks. (to Seraphin) Get on with it, neighbor.

SERAPHIN (sings)

I'm irrigating the canary.

PAUL (saucepan in hand)

And as for me,

I'm the cook of the lodging.

TOGETHER REFRAIN:

MIMI (putting on her shawl)

It's Mimi the grisette, etc.

PAUL AND SERAPHIN

It's Mimi the grisette, etc.

(Mimi leaves by the door at the back. Paul holds the saucepan over the fire. Seraphin gives water to the bird he's holding. They turn and look at each other and start laughing.)

BOTH

Ha! Ha! Ha! Ha!

SERAPHIN (aside)

What a stupid manner he has!

PAUL (aside)

What a fancy figure this character is cutting!

SERAPHIN (aside, observing him)

He's a rival; he's got all the symptoms.

PAUL (placing the remainder of the letter in the fire, aside)

Cursed letter—it almost ruined everything!

SERAPHIN

Swallow, beast! Open your beak! (aside) A future ministerial officer, in relations with such a bird!

PAUL (laughing)

It seems you don't listen very well down there.

SERAPHIN

Oh! If I gave him a tongue-lashing! (aside) And with you! No, let's use diplomacy—let's burrow within—it's not difficult, we process servers—we burrow within—very expertly.

PAUL (approaching, holding the milk and the saucepan)

Ah! Damn! My neighbor— For it seems we are all neighbors.

SERAPHIN (likewise, holding the canary)

It appears.

PAUL

You heard Miss Mimi—to do little chores for her, that's the way to please her.

SERAPHIN

And the gentleman hopes to charm her with the aid of this saucepan?

PAUL

Why not? Just like you serving as sommelier to these little gentlemen.

SERAPHIN

What little—? (noticing he is holding the canary still) Ah! (to the canary) That's enough of that, you drunk! Into your cell! (replaces the bird in its cage)

PAUL

And I. (placing the saucepan on the stove)

SERAPHIN (aside looking at Paul)

To the two of us now—the other canary! (aloud, with aplomb) Sir—I understand you—but I think I can affirm that Mimi doesn't love you.

PAUL

Bah—that's possible (aside) Bah! This imbecile— what's he know about it? (aloud) Then she loves—you?

SERAPHIN

Not more than anyone else. This opinion is the result of a series of observations—for although still young I've performed several studies on the heart of women. (sighing) Studies that were very dearly paid for!—ah!

PAUL

There! there! there!—and you think that—?

SERAPHIN

I maintain that a woman in love doesn't say, "Hold my milk over the fire—give my canary water," and other familiarities more or less whimsical. No, sir, no! A woman who loves—is touched, embarrassed, before the object of her palpitations, she blushes—the woman who loves—she stammers—the woman who—

PAUL

Really?

SERAPHIN

But, as for me, speaking to you, sir, I have been witness to a phenomenon even more plain! I knew a young woman of enormous education who composed extremely long poems.— Well, when she found herself in the presence of a blond gentleman she adored—she blurted out errors! Oh! Why, huge errors like a doorkeeper—which made your teeth gnash.

PAUL (gravely)

What! It went that far!

SERAPHIN

That far! Eh! My god! It's like our sex.

PAUL

What! Our sex!

SERAPHIN

Damn! I presume that you belong to mine. (singing)

In such a case, man is timid

Nerves agitated by love

He trembles by his Juliet

That he confronts with lowered eyes.

As for me, I've experienced it—when in love

What a funny face you make

What a dumb look.

PAUL (watching him)

Do you always need to be in love for that?

SERAPHIN

No—that's fair—no.

PAUL

Why, then, neighbor, if it's neither you, nor I, who does she love then?

SERAPHIN

Mimi? Why no—(stopping and aside) Oh, rakes of the regency, inspire me. (aloud) Why, everybody, sir!

PAUL

Everybody? (aside) Get out! That's what I was afraid of. (aloud) Are you really certain?

SERAPHIN

Everybody.—and nobody—you know the song. (singing)

Long live the grisettes

They are always "at home"—etc.

That's it! (giving himself big blows on his chest) Nothing, there, sir—nothing beneath the laces of the corset! I speak morally! Nothing! And as for me, me I thought to find here the model of a virtuous grisette! (with an air of resignation) I am going to take my leave and seek virtue in another section of the city. (aside) I have burrowed in!

PAUL

She has an air that's deceiving enough! Get out—it cannot be!

SERAPHIN

Ah! Ah! Ah! In that case ask Old Man Estragon, the doorkeeper, and Hortense his wife—they will tell you news about it! Nice news. (aside) I am going to corrupt them! I will consecrate to it a capital of six sous! (he goes to take his hat)

PAUL

What! These good folks—

**ESTRAGON (entering excitedly
and stopping at the back)**

This time there are two of them!

PAUL (turning)

Huh?

ESTRAGON (aside)

Ah! There's my man!—and he isn't forewarned!

PAUL

It's you, Papa Estragon? Everything going good?

ESTRAGON

Gentlemen, I am really yours—it's not going bad—Hortense either— (to Paul who looks at him) Hortense, my spouse. Pardon, Miss Pinson has gone out? I was bringing her her puce slippers—whose restoration I undertook in my spare time—on the quarter.

SERAPHIN (abruptly)

You should have given them back to her when she went by the lodge.

ESTRAGON

Heavens! (aside) He is vexed, so much the better. (aloud) I didn't notice her.

SERAPHIN

Come off it! You looked her over very carefully—old Lynx!

ESTRAGON (to Paul)

What's he calling me?

PAUL

He's calling you a concierge in English.

ESTRAGON

Ah! fine—I don't know a word of English. Ya, mien herr—two actually.

SERAPHIN

Say rather, that you are prying in the apartments of the tenants—to see what's going on.

ESTRAGON

And if that were so—I have the right. (aside) Wait a bit! I am going to fix you! (aloud) When the proprietor gave me the place of Lynx. (Seraphin laughs) What?—I can really speak English like you, perhaps, (resuming) he told me to watch over the morals—the morals, that's what he directed me to do most—after the stairways.

PAUL

And you busy yourself with it?

ESTRAGON

I scour them every morning.

SERAPHIN

Morals?

ESTRAGON (bewildered)

The stairways too!—what is it then? After that, you understand, it's your youth, which is nice and which gives you health! That's all! (pointing to a box) Ah! No, that's not it, that's Mr. Chaumont's box. Here's the object. (he goes to place the slippers on the table at the left) It's youth, I say, which lives alone and prefers to live together—hee, hee, hee! It's quite natural according to what my spouse says.

PAUL

Ah! Madame Estragon finds that—

ESTRAGON

Natural, yes— Then, as for me, I climb from time to time in the day to enlighten—like the lamp does the night, to make sure some man didn't slink into the little one's place.

PAUL

He slinks then?

(Seraphin coughs.)

ESTRAGON

He doesn't slink badly— You think, perhaps, that she lives only with her canaries? (Seraphin coughs) Ha! Ha! Ha!—it's not natural—as my wife says—(Seraphin coughs) Lord God! Do you have whooping cough?

SERAPHIN

No, no. (aside) Well, why he's doing very well—and gratis!

PAUL

Ah! Then, she isn't?

ESTRAGON (laughing)

No.

SERAPHIN (making signs to him)

Then, she is—

ESTRAGON

Yes, yes, yes.

SERAPHIN (to Paul)

That's plain! (he continues making signs)

PAUL (with regret)

What! My little neighbor—so frank—such a good kid.

ESTRAGON

Ah! Hell! These little ones, they play with the gents—that's playing with fire. (to Seraphin, who continues to make signs to him) Ah! God! Are you doing the Danse Macabre?

PAUL (aside)

Mimi—like the others!

ESTRAGON

That's playing with fire, I tell you, and one fine day, it's Hortense who told me this, she's as philosophic as a hoot-owl—one fine day, when the pot starts to boil—(excitedly) Ah! Lord! the milk starts to escape!

PAUL (running to the stove)

Devil! This concerns me.

SERAPHIN (low, shaking Estragon in his arms)

Old scoundrel!—you saved me ten sous!

ESTRAGON (baffled)

What! Ten sous? What are you talking about?

PAUL

Huh?

(They hear Mimi's voice.)

SERAPHIN (low)

Shut up, lynx, or I'll murder you.

MIMI (entering with bread)

Heavens! You were here, Papa Estragon?

PAUL (aside, looking at her)

It's a shame!

MIMI (screaming in the wings)

Yes, sir, yes, he's in my place—I am going to send him to you.

ESTRAGON

Who's asking for me?

MIMI

It's the young man on the first floor who's calling for you, shouting, treating you like—

ESTRAGON (excitedly)

Like?

MIMI

Anyway—a word that places you lower than the shoemakers!

SERAPHIN

Well-known!

ESTRAGON (furious, striding about)

Huh? That little Mr. Alfred.

PAUL

Alfred? (collecting himself) Ah, his name's Alfred.

ESTRAGON

Alfred Balissan—a little guy who is curled like a chicory, perfumed with eau de cologne—who spreads infection when he passes by. (to Mimi) Here are your puce slippers that I am bringing you—it's seventy-five centimes.

PAUL

Mr. Alfred? A young man who engages in intrigues—from what they say?

ESTRAGON

In intrigues? Yes! Yes!—and the proof is the other day a beautiful lady— (questioning himself) Must I say it? He gave me ten francs to keep my mouth shut— But, bah, I'm going—

MIMI

You are going to return him his money.

ESTRAGON

I am going to tell you everything. The other day a carriage stopped at our gate—and there was a little lady—blonde—

PAUL (aside)

It's really she.

ESTRAGON

Who prayed that Mr. Alfred come down.

SERAPHIN

He went down?

ESTRAGON

That's where you are mistaken; the little beggar replied that he was at home—he didn't seem to understand.

MIMI

And this lady?

ESTRAGON

She left, just the way she came.

PAUL (aside)

Oh! Yes!

ESTRAGON

But the next day, there she was again—on foot. This time, just when Mr. Alfred was coming in, I was hidden behind the door—and I heard, without wishing to.

SERAPHIN

Come off it!

ESTRAGON

No—sacred word—I heard the words of the little blonde: "Alfred, return them to me! Return them to me, Alfred!"

MIMI

What was it?

ESTRAGON

I don't know.

PAUL (aside)

As for me, I know.

ESTRAGON

To which he replied, the little curly-head: "Come up with me! Come look for them!"

SERAPHIN

And she went up?

PAUL (aside)

Oh! no!

ESTRAGON

On the contrary! She escaped again and the young man went in to his place all—

SERAPHIN

All frazzled.

ESTRAGON

Ah! I love that word— But, five minutes later a gentleman between the age of sixty and sixty-five— dappled grey, like me—was prowling around the house.

PAUL (aside)

Oh! Now, that's what I was afraid of!

SERAPHIN

It's the daddy!

MIMI

Or the husband!

ESTRAGON

And he comes every day, but the young lady never returns—although Mr. Alfred told me one night, with a mysterious air, "She's going to return."

SERAPHIN

She will return.

MIMI

Oh! I hope not!

PAUL (aside)

And me, too!

ESTRAGON

Eh! Don't stick your little hand in the fire. (singing)

Between you and me, I'm afraid the beauty

Might be at the end of her rope.

MIMI

Her husband?

ESTRAGON (singing)

Miss, I wouldn't want

To have my head in his hat.

His misfortune is going to be complete,

And he cannot squirm out of it.

Love is lying in wait to ruin her.

PAUL (aside)

And friendship to save her!

ESTRAGON

So much so that, this morning, the little curly-head was radiant and, indeed, he directed me to give him warning if I were to see the lady getting out of her carriage—towards noon—

PAUL (aside)

Noon—good.

ESTRAGON

But you are making me forget what I came here to do—for your puce slippers.

SERAPHIN (aside)

Old gossip.

ESTRAGON

Say, then, it's seventy-five centimes—because it's you! For this, I limp up six flights, to give Mademoiselle Blanchette her walking papers.

MIMI

Ah, my God!

PAUL

What? That pretty grisette that I saw the other day, decorated like a duchess?

SERAPHIN

And that I met the next day in a very short skirt, with a curtain in place of cashmere. (aside) Also— (looking at his dossier)

MIMI

Poor girl!

ESTRAGON

Completely hard up. She owes us three terms, 175 francs— But the move won't cost her much; the furniture's in hock.

SERAPHIN (aside)

By Jove!

MIMI

She's been seized?

ESTRAGON

In full! So much the better, says my wife, the philosopher—these little tenants—it's all riffraff!

MIMI (carrying her table)

Ah! Indeed! Thanks!

ESTRAGON

Not the women! Not the women!

SERAPHIN

Ah! Really! Thanks!

ESTRAGON

Not the men! We are only waiting for papers from the process server, to give her her eviction notice.

SERAPHIN (aside)

Ah! My God! I was forgetting about it! Let's see to this quickly. (taking his hat, to Paul) Are you coming, neighbor?

PAUL

No, no—I'm staying.

ESTRAGON

As for me, I'm going up.

SERAPHIN

As for me, I'm going down. (singing)

Soon, I hope

I'm going to work.

Nobody will suspect

I'm a process server's clerk.

ESTRAGON (singing)

Later, little mother.

I've got an iron heart

For the tenant

Who stops paying.

PAUL (singing)

Alone, in my room, my dear,

I'm going to be bored.

I'll have nothing to do.

I'm going to gossip.

MIMI (singing)

Seized by misery,

He's got a heart of steel.

He's an old Cerberus,

This porter.

ESTRAGON (returning)

It's seventy-five centimes, mamzelle!

SERAPHIN (aside)

Let's go release the errand boy.

REFRAIN TOGETHER

(Estragon and Seraphin leave.)

PAUL (aside)

Poor Emma!— But noon! I've got time. (looking at Mimi out of the corner of his eye) And I'm not sorry about that.

MIMI

Poor Blanchette!—where will she go?

PAUL

You are interested in that girl, Miss Mimi?

MIMI

Why not? You say correctly, because she isn't very well-behaved—that's possible. But you see, she has such a good heart! She gives everything she has—when she has something— The other week, again, she paid for ices for everyone on her landing.

PAUL

You were there?

MIMI (lowering her eyes)

No—I was ill.

PAUL

Sick!

MIMI (changing her tone)

And to say that there are fine gentlemen who smoke two-hundred-franc cigars that poison the streets! When all that is necessary is 175 francs to get her out of it!

PAUL

Eh! Who knows? Perhaps you will find one of those gentlemen.

MIMI

Ah! Don't believe it! Not on my landing, ever. (stamping her foot) God! How enraging it is to earn only thirty sous per day.

PAUL (stupefied)

Huh?— You only earn thirty sous per day, neighbor?

MIMI

Well! Why—isn't that nice?

PAUL

Thirty sous! (aside) They're right! There's something extra!

MIMI

One franc fifty! With that, you don't die of hunger. (resuming gaily) Ah! Yes, one dies of hunger—when you forget to have lunch— To table, neighbor. (she moves the table forward)

PAUL

To table— Here are my cherries.

MIMI

And here's my milk. (they sit down) Shall we share, if you like?

PAUL

Let's share—as the proverb says— "Give me what you have."

MIMI (finishing)

I will give you what I have.

(They eat.)

PAUL

Thirty sous per day, neighbor! And you are furnished like a princess!

MIMI

Well?

PAUL

And you dress like a flirt! That must cost a lot.

MIMI

You think so?

PAUL (singing)

What! This beautiful shawl that you wear on fest days?

MIMI (singing)

Go to the market, where they are found like fleece.

PAUL

What! These kerchiefs, this well-tailored dress?

MIMI

That's my work—and for good reason,

I don't charge for that.

PAUL

What! This bonnet, ravishing headdress,

Which sets off your pretty features so well?

MIMI

That costs me even less.

For it was God who gave me my face

And I made the bonnet myself.

PAUL (aside)

And to say with what a frank manner—of ingenuity—she's able—

MIMI

You aren't eating.

PAUL

Indeed— Do you know, neighbor, that you are very well disciplined, very reasonable? And that you would make a good little housekeeper?

MIMI

What!—I would make—but I already am a housekeeper!

PAUL

A household—of your own—it's incomplete— You need it.

MIMI

A set of chimney ornaments—Oh! Indeed—

PAUL (moving his chair closer to Mimi)

No—another thing.

MIMI (astonished)

Bah! I have a spoon, tongs, three chairs, a salad bowl, a cake plate, a mirror—

PAUL (getting very close to her)

Keep going. (very low) A lover!

MIMI

A lover! Ha, ha, ha!

PAUL

He must present himself.

MIMI

Enormously! First of all, all my neighbors—that's in the queue—I've been adored by the whole landing—with sighs—that make the house tremble.

PAUL

And on your side.

MIMI

Oh, as for me, I laugh with them—but when they want to laugh too much—I don't laugh.

PAUL (observing her)

What! Never one of them, bolder than the others.

MIMI

Oh! Indeed—they are all very bold, there's one especially, wait, the one who was living in your room before you. One night he played the farce of breaking down the communicating door—that one—and falling in here like a sudden shower.

PAUL

Ah! Bah! And you shouted for help!

MIMI

Shout? To be a shrew? Those who are afraid scream.

PAUL

What did you do?

MIMI

Nothing.

PAUL

What did you say?

MIMI

I didn't say anything—but, what I know is that he became ashamed, asked my pardon—with big tears in his eyes.

PAUL (aside, rising)

If it were true! But no—all that I've just learned.

MIMI (rising, too)

And the next day, didn't he want to marry me, for real!

PAUL (helping Mimi replace the table)

And you told him?

MIMI

I told him—first of all—to get the door fixed, and after that to go get married elsewhere. He was a nice young man, I don't say—but if you think I will take the first to come along! Ah! But with my little air—I was raised to be more well-to-do than I am.

PAUL

Meaning, if you were to find—?

MIMI

I'm not looking—and then husbands, they don't have many on my landing. But, bah! I am in no rush—when one comes along, we will see. (singing)

As for lovers, I'm on my guard.

Men are very prompt to change,

And as for a husband that heaven is keeping for me,

I'm waiting for him here without bothering.

I'm not alone, I think,

I have two companions, see here. (pointing to the bird cage)

My canaries give me patience

While waiting until I have a husband. (repeat refrain)

(She hangs the cage in the window.)

PAUL

So, you don't perceive that you lack—someone?

MIMI

Well, indeed—there are moments when I have to take work to town and when it rains.

PAUL

Ah, you are counting on making your husband carry?

MIMI

Who else?

PAUL

That's fair; the right belongs to him.

MIMI

Happily, the weather is good today, and I am not going far. (aside, placing bonnets in a carton) Poor Blanchette, if I were able to help her!

PAUL

What! You are leaving?

MIMI

You'll watch my room, won't you?

(Mimi gets herself ready before a little mirror over the chest of drawers.)

PAUL

I—I'd really like to—but you mustn't absent yourself for long, because—I can really agree to that—what Papa Estragon was saying—about the little lady, you know? That piques my curiosity.

MIMI (looking at him)

Heaven!

PAUL (forcing himself to laugh)

Ha, ha, ha, ha—that's funny!

MIMI (dressing)

You aren't going to laugh like that, you too? a woman who has a husband—jealous, maybe!

PAUL

Certainly!

MIMI

Huh?

PAUL (catching himself)

I suppose—

MIMI

And who knows!—children—

PAUL (forgetting himself)

Exactly.

MIMI

Huh?

PAUL (catching himself)

I suppose.

MIMI

And now there's a bad household—misfortunes—perhaps orphans. Ah! Look, Mr. Paul, that seizes my heart, mine! And to prevent such a disaster—(almost weeping) Oh, if she was here—I would say to her—Madame—

PAUL (very interested)

Yes, yes.

MIMI

It's wrong—because! And then—you have duties—and then—

PAUL (the same)

Yes, yes.

MIMI (turning about and laughing)

Ha! Ha! Ha!—this air, you take me in— Does it concern you now? Rather, give me my shawl.

PAUL (taking a Tartan hanging at the back)

Here, neighbor, here.

MIMI

Wait, sir—don't look. (she throws the shawl over her head)

PAUL

Oh! Why—

MIMI

It's more secure—be nice about it. (she changes the kerchief)

PAUL

Say, I'm bored over it—I am all alone—if there was a little hole to see.

MIMI

It's finished. (Paul removes the shawl) Here, raise my neck a bit—attach the shawl with these big pins—careful not to prick me.

PAUL

Don't worry. (aside, looking at her neck) Ah! My word—the opportunity makes the— (he kisses her)

MIMI (uttering a little scream)

Ah!

PAUL

Did I prick you, my neighbor?

MIMI (completely shocked)

No, no, you didn't prick me—but all the same, you didn't attach my shawl. (making a face at him) Fie! Sir, you are the first—

PAUL

Really?

MIMI (taking the box)

Goodbye, neighbor.

PAUL

See you later, neighbor.

MIMI (returning)

Why, I think so!—you are going to be bored all by yourself. I cannot offer you the books of my library. (suddenly) Ah! A good idea! would you like me to forgive you? Would you like to be nice, yes? Well, amuse yourself by sweeping my room.

PAUL

Huh?

MIMI

Sweep, neighbor, sweep hard—that will amuse you.

(Mimi leaves.)

PAUL (alone)

Ah, indeed, for goodness sake, I wasn't expecting that! Sweep hard! I really want to eat some cherries and attach the shawl—that I really like—attaching the shawl—but sweeping up—ha, ha, ha— This little one is astonishing—the devil take me, I'm terrified to forget—(resuming with comic gravity) Be proud, Baron Paul Duflot—noble since yesterday, baron of commerce and industry—that's what! Who was your father, if you please? A poor little commission merchant, who married a little working girl, a grisette, like your neighbor—and that grisette was his whole life. (sighing) Ah! In a way that Mimi Pinson won't ever be! My mother had for her dowry virtue, a righteousness proof against all, and (sighing) it seems that Mimi is consuming her dowry before marriage. (changing tone) Come on, come on, it was to think like that that I made myself a commission merchant and that I am living here on the fifth floor. Oh no—to save a woman and to cure a jealous husband of his suspicions—and, then, after that—(looking about him) Goodbye, poor little attic—goodbye, my sweet Mimi—I will no longer hear you say, "Neighbor," (laughing despite himself) "sweep my room!" Since there's no way of getting out of it, it must be done under pain of passing for—what I am. (seeing a broom and a stick) Here are the necessary instruments. (going to the window) I notice in the street a commissioner, a provincial— Ah! Yes, the street! She's very far away. (he leans out the window)

SERAPHIN (entering, to himself)

I got rid of the errand boy and— (aloud) Still, here!

PAUL

Huh? (aside) Oh! The provincial was asking questions! Wait, wait—I am going to make you sweep, you!

SERAPHIN

Our neighbor left?

PAUL

Yes—and I am going to beg you to do something—which may disturb you a bit—because I promised Mamzelle Mimi to sweep her room.

SERAPHIN

Bah! You are charged with it. (aside) Ha, ha, ha, ha! I don't envy your duties. (sits to the right)

PAUL

And if she is satisfied, (low and gaily) I'll have two kisses for my reward. Ah! But! I don't like this way of rewarding her sweeper! She can be economical—but I don't like it!

SERAPHIN

Two kisses—a payment of—(aside) Why, I don't—

PAUL

Also, I feel a passion in me. (he sweeps clumsily)

SERAPHIN (still seated, sneering)

Oh, oh, oh!

PAUL (stopping)

What?

SERAPHIN

Nothing, nothing—I am snickering quietly so as not to interrupt you.

PAUL

And—why are you snickering?

SERAPHIN (disdainfully)

Where did you learn to sweep?

PAUL

Why—I think I'm accustomed to it.

SERAPHIN

Yes, I believe you are accustomed—to sweep clumsily. First of all, this leg—ha, ha, ha! One would say you were going to dance the Mazurka in a ballroom.

PAUL

And this here?

SERAPHIN

Ah! Good! You are going to make a big split, like a ballet dancer!

PAUL (shuffling his feet)

Here! Here!

SERAPHIN

Fine! Fine! He's running about! They'd say that you were shuffling the cards with your feet.

PAUL

Come on! You wouldn't do it any differently.

SERAPHIN

Me? Me? (aside) Innocent! If you scrubbed your clerk's room every Sunday!

PAUL

No, no! I bet you don't understand anything about how to do it!

SERAPHIN (rising)

I could—ah! Bravo! He's going to kick himself out the door. One could, without being of the best strength, give you a lesson.

PAUL

You?

SERAPHIN

Me!

PAUL

I defy you to.

SERAPHIN

Ah! You defy me to. (swinging the stick, fitting the brush, and scrubbing with all his strength) There, there! That's how you do it! That's how you scrub in the grand salons! Follow with your eye, follow the motion.

PAUL (relaxing on a chair to the left)

Bad.

SERAPHIN

Bad? (redoubling his efforts) Why, take a look before speaking! Observe this right leg! There's some steam in it!

PAUL

Execrable!

SERAPHIN

Execrable? Why, wretch, jealousy is carrying you away! (dancing on the brush) Ah! That's bad? Come on? There! There! Ah! That's execrable? There, again! There! There! There!

PAUL

Bravo!

SERAPHIN (dancing on the brush)

See, if you please,

How gamely, how supple!

Like a jade,

I stride over the floor.

PAUL

Yes, you've got some talent,

My dear boy, I confess it.

SERAPHIN

See how it shines.

Do it better if you can.

PAUL

Neighbor, I am conquered, humiliated.

SERAPHIN

No breeze, graceful method.

There you are!

Imitate it.

PAUL

Me? Never in my life.

Scrub, scrub, you were born to do it.

TOGETHER

SERAPHIN

See, if you please,

How gamely, how supple,

Like a jade

I stride over the floor!

By slouching,

You slide with softness.

See how it shines.

Do it better if you can.

PAUL

Neighbor, it's perfect.

How gamely, how supple,

Like a jade

Sliding over the floor.

Yes, he's got some talent,

My dear boy, I confess it.

And truly, never

Will I do better.

SERAPHIN (releasing the brush, the broom, and falling stretched out onto a chair)

Ah, I cannot do any more. I must be red as a lobster—boiled. (he stretches out while Paul disposes of the tools)

MIMI (entering)

Here I am, here I am—I wasn't long, was I, huh? (seeing Paul still holding the broom) Ah! My neighbor! What! You had the kindness—ah! How sweet that was of you.

SERAPHIN (misunderstanding)

Oh! It's such a little thing.

MIMI

How hot he is!—this poor lad! Oh! (offering him her cheek) Come! Kiss me for your trouble.

SERAPHIN (rising hurriedly)

She said—

PAUL (kissing her)

One—and two.

SERAPHIN

He has her number! He has it! (shouting) But doggone it! It was me—over here!

MIMI (to Seraphin)

See what it is, neighbor, to be good and obliging! That deserves something.

SERAPHIN (still shouting)

Why, I'm robbed! It's as if he took two kisses from my pocket! (to Mimi) If I say to you—

MIMI

Damn! Earn them in your turn—lazy, sitting there on a chair.

(Seraphin wants to speak.)

PAUL (cutting off his words)

Lazy! Sitting there on a chair.

MIMI

Here, so you can relieve stiffness of your legs.

SERAPHIN

Damnation! They are sufficiently relieved. They are torpid. (to Mimi) Why, it's—

MIMI

You don't know? A nasty little clerk of a bailiff, who's bringing a paper against Blanchette—to think we cannot save her! One hundred seventy-five francs—and all I can do is weep.

PAUL (aside)

Poor girl!—that's it indeed!

MIMI

And that made me forget the chickweed for the canaries. (to Seraphin) Say then, go down to the grocer for me—that will make me ten flights— Your turn, now!

SERAPHIN

Yes, count down. (aside) She will give me something like she gave to the other again, for my trouble.

MIMI

Well?

SERAPHIN

Pardon, neighbor—I had a political discussion with the grocer and we are cold to each other. Besides, I haven't dined.

(He looks at Paul.)

MIMI

Hum!—good-for-nothing!

SERAPHIN (aside)

Good to scrub, that's all!

PAUL

Neighbor, I accept the commission. (aside) Soon I'll have to buy two or three francs worth of chickweed.

MIMI

You are not too worn out?

PAUL (taking his hat)

Me? Oh! My God, it's as if I hadn't done a thing.

SERAPHIN (aside)

He allows himself this nonsense again! (to Mimi) We have a score to settle and when you are alone—

MIMI

Hello, hello! (recalling Paul) Ah! Say, I think that the little curly-head is waiting for someone—he's lying in wait.

PAUL (aside)

Oh! I will speak to him!

MIMI

He has a vexed air!

SERAPHIN

I really think so, if kisses take place in front of his nose—like mine.

PAUL (to Mimi)

Are you coming, neighbor? (singing) To obey you, I rush,

Happy to save you steps. (aside)

I will be able, without appearing to,

Learn what is taking place below.

SERAPHIN (low to Paul)

See, how familiar she is.

What lack of manners—no sincerity.

You can be sure a woman doesn't love

A man she sends for chickweed.

TOGETHER

PAUL

To obey you, I rush, etc.

SERAPHIN (aside)

Vainly he rushes to please her.

The wretch will waste his steps.

The doctrine that I profess

Tells me she doesn't love him.

MIMI

How sweet he is—what a hurry he's in.

He's trying to save my steps.

It's to little cares like these that virtue

Often cannot resist.

(They leave.)

MIMI

Ah! Now that I'm alone here.—(she goes back to work. Estragon rushes in and locks the door) Huh? Ah! My God! What's the matter with you? your eyes are popping out of your head!

ESTRAGON

There's something to make them pop! A proud news, go on!

MIMI (coming closer)

Ah! Bah!—is it amusing?

ESTRAGON

It's thrilling! While coming down from Blanchette, whom we have just notified of the seizure of her goods—

MIMI

Are you still boasting of that—! Poor girl!

ESTRAGON

I met on the stairs a servant in a red vest—a groom—

MIMI

A groom. (pronounces it "gru-um")

ESTRAGON

It's written g-r-o-o-m—it's pronounced groom! He was examining all the doors on the landing. "Who do you want, groom?" He looked at me as if I were stupid.

MIMI

I understand that.

ESTRAGON

The name didn't come. He showed me a letter he was bearing for one of the young men of the landing—he didn't want to let it go, but what did I read on the address?

MIMI

To Mr. Paul or Mr. Seraphin?

ESTRAGON

To Baron Duflot!

MIMI

Heavens!

ESTRAGON

To Monsieur le Baron.

MIMI

Duflot. (troubled) Are you quite sure of that?

ESTRAGON

Heavens! You've got all upset, like me! And even Hortense! She will be suffocated—we have a baron on the fifth floor!

MIMI

Him! Mr. Duflot!

ESTRAGON

A baron at three hundred francs rent, and without straw matting! Sonofabitch! It's some remnant of the old regime.

MIMI (to herself)

Eh! No—that cannot be! And why here? Would he know?

ESTRAGON

You know him?

MIMI

Me? Yes—no, that is to say—which one? Ah! Yes, ah, yes—Mr. Paul, Mr. Seraphin—which one? (shouting) Wait! I am there! No, both of them have glazed boots.

ESTRAGON

You've got it?

MIMI (to herself)

Yes! The subterfuges that he told me about his situation, that bouquet, and then his refusal to go for chickweed.

ESTRAGON

For chickweed—what?

MIMI

Ah!

ESTRAGON

Ah!

MIMI

And that letter Mr. Paul burned, and that he took from his papers! That letter to Baron—

ESTRAGON

He's the big one?

MIMI

No.

ESTRAGON

He's the little one?

MIMI

He's—

ESTRAGON

He's—?

MIMI (seeing Seraphin enter)

Ah! There he is!

ESTRAGON

Oh! (they both stand motionless)

SERAPHIN

Neighbor—you are alone and I am coming to—(seeing her frozen and embarrassed) Eh! Well? What's the matter with you?

MIMI (stammering)

Me? Why—I—I don't know—ask Mr. Estragon.

SERAPHIN

(looking at him in his turn) Heavens! What's wrong with him, too, Papa Lynx.

ESTRAGON

Me? Why, I—I don't know. Ask— (he makes questioning signs to Mimi, if this is the baron. She replies the same way. Yes, yes, and makes signals him to leave.)

ESTRAGON

Understood.

SERAPHIN (staring at them)

Ah! Indeed, why it's…hieroglyphics?

ESTRAGON

There he goes speaking English again. (to Mimi) Yes, yes. (he leaves with exaggerated bows, then stops at the back) This is going to turn Hortense topsy-turvy from top to bottom. (Seraphin turns and makes more exaggerated bows.)

(Exit Estragon.)

SERAPHIN (returning the bows)

Mr. Estragon, I really have the honor. Ha! Ha! Ha!

MIMI (forcing herself to laugh)

Ha! Ha! Ha! (aside) In fact, I prefer that this be he than the other one!

SERAPHIN

What's got him, Mr. Hortense, huh?

MIMI (still embarrassed)

Damn!—as for me—I—(excitedly) Take the trouble to be seated. (she brings a chair which she dusts with her table cloth)

SERAPHIN (speechless)

Goodness! Goodness! Goodness! Goodness!

MIMI (Aside, abruptly)

Ah! Lord God! As for me, who made him give my canaries water to drink. (aloud) Sir.

SERAPHIN

Sir? (aside) What a way she's looking at me.

MIMI

If I had known—certainly—

SERAPHIN

Why, she's blushing a lot! Is this going to continue a bit?

MIMI

I would never have dared—because you—as for me that—

SERAPHIN (the same)

Why she's stammering tremendously—! Symptom!

MIMI

I would never have thought—hav't' beg you—

SERAPHIN (jumping)

A—A blunder! A real blunder! (explosively) I am loved!

MIMI

Huh?

SERAPHIN

No, no, nothing— Don't pay any attention.

(aside, exalted) It's come—there it is—think of it! Now there's the blunder demanded!—we are there. (aloud) But, pardon, pardon, neighbor—a change like this—so sudden at a moment when one was not expecting it—for in the end—what's it mean?

MIMI (timidly)

You know very well.

SERAPHIN

I suspect it. (aside) Eyes lowered, heart in her mouth—she's taken—oh darling, go!

MIMI

It's that—you are no longer the same for me!

SERAPHIN (aside)

That's it!—oh, how I'm palpitating!

MIMI

Since now that I know—

SERAPHIN

What?

MIMI

Who you are.

SERAPHIN

Who I—(aside) Sonofabitch! The bailiff is unveiled.

MIMI

Why have you hidden it from me, sir?

SERAPHIN (interrupting her)

Because I was afraid of displeasing you, oh Mimi—but, now that you know everything—I no longer intend to hide anything— Well, yes, I was deceiving you—I am one of them!

MIMI (triumphant)

Ah!

SERAPHIN

You know my secret— In your turn—you owe me a confession!

MIMI (troubled)

Me? Oh heaven—you know?

SERAPHIN

I've guessed everything! Your emotion—this unease, this blunder—I know everything!

MIMI

You know that I am—

SERAPHIN

Yes.

MIMI

Your cousin?

SERAPHIN (startled)

Huh? (aside) A cousin, now!

MIMI

Ah! My God! You didn't know it!

SERAPHIN

No! that is to say, yes—that is to say, no. (aside) Ah, why, I'm no longer with it!

MIMI

I didn't say anything—you've learned nothing. No, no, it's not for she who is poor to recall the relative who is rich—

SERAPHIN

You are saying? (aside) I am rich, now? I am rich and I have a cousin! Ah! Why, that's how we are stuttering! I stutter, she stutters, we stut—

MIMI

Ah! What a thought!

SERAPHIN

What, again?

MIMI

You couldn't hide yourself to do ill—on the contrary—I am sure that your title serves you only to do good.

SERAPHIN

My title—indeed—yes—sometimes. (aside) What's she take bailiffs for anyway?

MIMI (aside)

He's not proud of being a baron—that's nice! (aloud) Therefore, I prefer you to tell you everything plainly, Mr. Seraphin—you are generous and good—you ought to be when you are rich.

SERAPHIN

Certainly, I— (aside) There she goes again!

MIMI

I know—for a long while—that you love to help the wretched.

SERAPHIN

Damn! When one can— (aside) Right to the last decimal point!

MIMI

Well!—here—just now I was all atremble, and now I feel courageous. (getting excited) Come on, then! If it didn't cost a bit, it wouldn't be meritorious—(with persuasion) My cous—

SERAPHIN

Huh?

MIMI (resuming)

Sir—you know, there is—in this house—a poor, sick, girl—

SERAPHIN

La Blanchette on the sixth.

MIMI

Come to her assistance—pay for her.

SERAPHIN

Huh? (aside) I, who just caused— (gesture of kicking her out the door)

MIMI (continuing)

Perhaps you will save her from a greater danger! Oh, that will be money very well placed—really!

SERAPHIN

Yes! Yes! Yes!— And you will love me?

MIMI

I will adore you!

SERAPHIN

Oh! I consent to it.

MIMI

Well! Go—bring your help to her yourself, to receive her blessings.

PAUL (entering carrying an enormous sack of chickweed)

Here's the chickweed requested.

SERAPHIN

Ah! Heaven—there's enough for all the canaries in Paris!

MIMI (running to remove Paul's hat and throwing the chickweed on the floor)

Will you take your hat off?

PAUL

What's up?

MIMI

Before him!

PAUL

Who?

MIMI

Hush! I will tell you.

PAUL (abruptly)

Ah, indeed, neighbor, you will explain to me.

MIMI (resting her hand on his mouth)

Stop!

SERAPHIN (low to Paul)

Did I tell you she adored someone—and it wasn't you!

SERAPHIN (low to Mimi)

I am going to go find the money.

MIMI

Go, baron.

PAUL

Huh?

SERAPHIN (aside)

Baron! Could it be, without my suspecting it—could they have been abusing me since my birth?

TOGETHER

SERAPHIN AND PAUL (aside)

Ah, I am indeed

Speechless, stupefied.

What is this secret,

This mystery?

But as for me, everything's fine.

Prudently, we say nothing.

The way to happiness

Is to keep your mouth shut.

MIMI (aside)

See, how he seems,

Speechless, stupefied;

Of his title he made

A mystery.

(Exit Seraphin.)

MIMI

You don't know! he's a baron!

PAUL

Ah! Bah!

MIMI

Baron Duflot.

PAUL

Ah! Bah!

MIMI

He admitted it.

PAUL

Ah! Bah!

MIMI

God! What a stupid look you have— If I tell you so—a disguise—a whole scandal.

PAUL

And this Baron Duflot, he is?

MIMI

He is Mr. Seraphin.

PAUL (bursting out)

Ah! That's a bit much!

MIMI

And why's that? Well! I don't know—I had an idea of it—that face, those distinguished manners. (Paul chokes back a laugh) Go on, laugh! I know something about it, perhaps— And another proof.

PAUL

Ah! Let's see, another proof?

MIMI

It's he who's going to find money—175 francs—for the sixth term.

PAUL

Him! (aside) Ah! He won't do me out of this good deed!

MIMI

You say?

PAUL

I say that it's wrong of you not to address yourself to me, not to have asked me.

MIMI (choking back a burst of laughter)

My turn to laugh, for goodness sake. Put on your airs! Do you have more money than I do?

PAUL

It's true—it's true.

MIMI

Whereas he?

PAUL

He, Baron—Baron Duflot— Oh! Oh!

MIMI

Well! Look—they told me that he was an original—that he'd placed his baron's title in his pocket—that he had refused great marriages—and that he had remained all simple, like his father—I didn't want to believe it—

PAUL

You knew his father?

MIMI

Now, I know everything.

PAUL

Yes, yes—and the rest goes all alone—a baron, a moneybags, who comes to lodge near your nest—it's he who wants to get close to you.

MIMI

You are there!

PAUL

It's he who loves you.

MIMI

That's true.

PAUL

It's he who offers you his heart.

MIMI

That's clear.

PAUL

His fortune.

MIMI

Don't want it.

PAUL

His hand.

MIMI

Don't take it— Well! Yes, take it, shake it, and say to him Thanks! We cannot do it.

PAUL (with an air of doubt)

Ah! Don't you believe it!

MIMI

Ah! Not believe it?—because he's a baron and rich, does that prevent him from being ugly and stupid?

PAUL

Rich—noble—you wouldn't love him?

MIMI

Heavens! Suppose I loved another!

PAUL (excitedly)

Another? Who then?

MIMI

That's none of your concern.

PAUL

But—

MIMI

But—now noon is coming—rather speak to me of the little woman—that's waiting on the first.

PAUL

She won't come, I hope.

MIMI

What's it to you?

PAUL

Nothing—nothing— It's that leaving the grocer, I saw the husband on guard duty—I recognized him.

MIMI

Huh? You?

PAUL

Oh! He's only a husband, you see, that's recognizable right away—it gives you an air. (listening) Oh heaven!—don't you hear it—a carriage! (running to the window)

MIMI

It's she—she is ruined.

PAUL

No, no—the carriage is passing by.

MIMI

So much the better—my heart was gripped.

PAUL

And me, too! Poor woman! Still, that doesn't concern me—I laugh about it—and yet, I want to save her.

MIMI

Ah, yes—but the means? If one could trap the husband—jealous villain—make him think—

PAUL

I understand what you mean.

MIMI

Ah! That's fortunate—as for me, I don't.

PAUL

Indeed. (aside) I'll wait for her—I'll warn her, and—

MIMI

Ah! My God—that man there—down there—

PAUL

That's the husband.

MIMI

Impossible that he won't see his wife arrive. Ah! An idea—if we were to tell everything to Baron Duflot—he might be able—

PAUL

Nothing! The husband detests him—he is jealous of him.

MIMI

Ah! Bah!—who told you?

PAUL

Silence!

ESTRAGON (entering)

Well, well! Now there's a famous one! It's over.

MIMI

Over—what?

PAUL

Did she arrive?

ESTRAGON

Lord God! I didn't see you—I was afraid—(aside) He made a lease with her?

PAUL

Speak—you say?

ESTRAGON

I say that now there's a famous—wait, miz, wait!

MIMI

What is it?

ESTRAGON

The receipt I am taking to little Blanchette.

MIMI

The receipt?

ESTRAGON

Since I've received the money! That the same groom just deposited in my lodging on behalf of an unknown person.

PAUL (going to the window)

Ah! If this is all.

ESTRAGON

What do you mean! What's this?

PAUL (aside)

Heavens! A carriage! It's she!

(He leaves without being perceived.)

ESTRAGON

What's this! One hundred seventy-five francs.

MIMI

He was able to do it—good young man! (suddenly) My God! What an uproar! What is it I hear?

ESTRAGON (at the back)

Oh! Some company!—one would say a battle on the stairway.

A VOICE (outside)

Hippolyte!

ESTRAGON

And Hortense is calling me! (shouting) Here, my darling! (leaving) Sonofabitch! If it was a thief! (he leaves, the uproar increases)

MIMI (at the back)

Ah! I think so!— Yes, it was! (Mimi looking out the back)

(The blocked door is forcibly shaken; it gives way, and suddenly opens, and Paul rushes in Mimi's room)

PAUL (to an unseen person)

Come.

MIMI (turning)

Heaven!

PAUL (low)

Wait. (excitedly to Mimi) I am pursued—creditors—help!

MIMI

You— Then it's for that—

PAUL

That I was hiding myself— Yes! Listen—on the stairway. (while Mimi listens at the back) Get in here quick!

(He makes a veiled woman enter; the lady is hidden in the alcove without being seen.)

MIMI (excitedly)

They are rapping at your door. (rapping can be heard) They are going to break it in. There's some shouting— "I heard him."

PAUL

It's the bailiff! Go in there.— You are at home and you don't know me.

MIMI

Great idea! I, who do not love the bailiffs. Indeed, what I will say is, this is my room—what is it you want?

PAUL

Yes, yes—that's the thing—quick!

MIMI

Don't worry—I am going to stop them— You, run away by my door.

(She goes into Paul's room, who holds open the door leading to his room, and casts the following words at the veiled lady.)

PAUL (excitedly)

You are saved! Take this purse, go up one floor—to the sixth—a poor unfortunate girl is sick— You came into this house for a work of charity—without stopping at the first—nor at my place—I didn't see you—I was in my room.

(The uproar increases. He quickly goes back into his room and shuts the door. The lady starts to leave, when Estragon opens the door at the back and pops his head in. The veiled lady only has time to rush into Mimi's alcove. All this happens simultaneously and very fast.)

ESTRAGON (laughing at the door

as he enters without looking)

Don't be afraid of anything, Miz Mimi—it's the husband—the ash grey-colored one—followed by all the tenants! He caught his spouse—according to what he said—not on the first floor. It seems he pursued her even to the door of Mr. Paul. As for me, I didn't see a thing—but he heard a woman's voice— (imitating) Ah! I am ruined! Come! This is going to be fun! (entering suddenly) Heavens! Where are you then?—There isn't anyone. (going towards the Alcove) Miz Mimi! (running to the door at back) Everybody's out!

PAUL (opening the blocked door)

At last—she was able to escape.

ESTRAGON (turning back)

Ah! Bah! Ah! Heavens! Ah! Fine!—the house is famous today, now! And the lady who was there in your room—?

PAUL

Huh? What lady? I don't know.

MIMI (coming back from Paul's by the same door, and quite troubled)

Why, no—it was not a bailiff.

ESTRAGON

Ah! Bah! Ah! Heavens!— Ah! Fine!— That woman's voice, in your place—it was Miz Mimi!

MIMI

Me?— What do you mean?

PAUL (to Estragon)

Leave!—Leave!

ESTRAGON

Yes—I'm off. (aside) Excuse me, little lady. (aloud) But the other one?

PAUL (pushing him)

Will you get out of here. (returning, aside) He didn't see her leave.

MIMI (very upset)

But am I to know at last what this signifies? Those creditors—they were all tenants in this house— There you were in your room with me—so you had nothing to fear? And, seeing us alone, they all left in a manner—which has me all upset. And then that gentleman who was so furious and who stopped and took off his hat to me and apologized saying, "You are not she!"— He was searching for someone who wasn't there— Then who was it, Mr. Paul? How upset you are! As for me, I don't know what I am experiencing— Who was it?

(At this moment the lady emerges from the alcove and rapidly sneaks out. Mimi, who has seen her, lets out a little scream.)

MIMI

Ah!

PAUL

You know everything. (taking her hands effusively) This secret—it's a good deed—that I am sharing with you! This lady, who is leaving here, is the daughter of my tutor—of the man who was my second father, she was a sister to me! Chained, despite herself, to a despotic and jealous husband, who never wanted to see me, she was unable to resist the seductions, which were torn from her letters—with which they hoped to ruin her completely—which would have ruined her! If I, the friend of the family, had not, for the last week, watched over her to save her!

MIMI

Eight days? You entered here?

PAUL (continuing)

If, at the moment when her husband, crossed the sill of this house, I had not dragged her, almost dying, up here, into my room— (Mimi looks at him with excitement) The room of a brother. (resuming) Unfortunately—the noise of our steps—my door locking—a cry of terror—attracted this man to your landing—he summoned me to open—he was going to force the door! He doesn't know me—but his wife in my room—pale, trembling—what to say? Happily, she was able to escape through here—while you deceived him—I am breathing—I am happy! (looking at her, astonished) But—you?

MIMI

Me? Yes—no question. (singing)

Just like you, it's a joy for me

To have saved this—imprudent—woman.

And yet, I feel, in my heart,

A suspicion, despite myself, which troubles and torments me.

What! You so good. (resuming) Oh! No I don't want to believe it. (begging)

But, tell me, sir, from the bottom of your soul,

How could you preserve the honor of this woman

Without saving hers at the price of mine?

PAUL (confused)

Mimi!—why—I thought.

SERAPHIN (entering with Estragon who he has by the collar)

You were their accomplice, old pirate.

ESTRAGON (shouting)

Let go of my collar—you'll rip it, Baron!

SERAPHIN (releasing him)

Baron yourself! This is a shame! It's for this I was gotten rid of, sending me to the sixth floor to bear my savings—175 francs—and to receive blessings. I received them! With this lady!

PAUL (excitedly)

This lady!—she was—

SERAPHIN (abruptly)

As for you, I'm not talking to you. (to Mimi in a soft tone) This door is blocked and if ever it is open—(explosively) It's open!

ESTRAGON

That it is!

MIMI (timidly)

But, sir—

SERAPHIN

Go, go, listen to the neighbors—and especially the women—and this gentleman in pursuit of his wife—who he found upstairs—the imbecile!

PAUL

Great God—he found her—

SERAPHIN (more forcefully)

I am not speaking to you. (continuing) And the whole house who surprised you with this gentleman—

MIMI

Ah!

ESTRAGON

It's true.

SERAPHIN (reproachfully)

In a room—belonging to another sex! You, Mamzelle, who proclaimed righteousness, even virtue!—without a single lover—not one.

PAUL

What do I hear?

MIMI

But I swear to you that this is unworthy—that—

SERAPHIN

Quit it! Perhaps you think that I am going to make a gull of a husband, like this one who's going to ask pardon of his wife—

PAUL (joyfully)

Truly—he's asking her.

SERAPHIN (in a rage)

I am not speaking to you! (to Mimi) And as for me, who loved you—me, who gave water to your canaries—me, who wanted to offer you my heart, my hand—and—my hand!

ESTRAGON

Ah! Bah! A baron.

PAUL

The Devil! It's an honor.

MIMI

That I would have refused, and that I will refuse again. (to Seraphin) Yes, sir, yes, your title, your fortune, do I care about that? Me? Did I ever think about it? And still it's not necessary to be so vain about it—I am your cousin, after all!

SERAPHIN

There she goes again!

PAUL AND ESTRAGON

His cousin!

MIMI

Mima Pinsonier—your mother's niece—and because my father wasn't as lucky as yours in his manufacturing—because he wasn't made a baron like yours—

SERAPHIN

Why, no!

PAUL (very moved)

Keep on going!

MIMI (continuing)

There's no need to think I am less proud than you—ah! Indeed—I am refusing you, rich as you are, baron as you are.

SERAPHIN

No, indeed.

PAUL

Very fine!

ESTRAGON

She refuses.

MIMI (the same)

What I want in my husband—if I take one—is that he be a fine lad, neither noble nor stupid—I don't insist on that—it's that he protect me, rather than condemn me! It's that he believe me, when I tell him I am an honest girl! It's that he esteem me! It's that he love me!—here, with all his heart!

PAUL

Like me.

MIMI (carried away)

Yes, Mr. Paul, like you.

ESTRAGON

Oh! What a mistake!

MIMI (the same)

Because you judge me better! Because you have placed me by half in a good deed! That consoles me for everything, and I am not unsaying it now. (she takes him by the arm) Let the door be open— It's no longer my place, it's no longer your place—it's both our places! I can resume gaily my needlework and my songs, and laugh at the spying of porters.

ESTRAGON

Huh?

MIMI

The concerns of the neighborhood and the great fury of The Baron.

SERAPHIN

No, indeed!

PAUL (laughing)

Bravo!—my wife!

ESTRAGON (laughing)

Instead of being baroness—

SERAPHIN (shaking him by the collar)

If you say that word one more time I'll break your skull.

ESTRAGON

Let go of my collar!

SERAPHIN (shouting)

But she won't be a baroness—because I am not a baron!—but what rage to rub in my face a title, me, Seraphin Moutonnet, bailiff's clerk.

MIMI

Bailiff's clerk!

SERAPHIN

I've let the cat out of the bag.

MIMI

O fie! Ah! Yuck!

ESTRAGON

Quit it! And the groom and the tenant on the sixth! There's a baron in the house, for sure!—I have to have one.

SERAPHIN

It's not me!

ESTRAGON

Nor me.

MIMI

Why, who is it then?

PAUL (pointing to Seraphin)

Hell—it's got to be one of the two of us.

(Mimi Pinson looks at him and timidly withdraws her arm from his.)

ESTRAGON

Ah! Pooh!

SERAPHIN

A baron, him? (disdainfully) Ah! Fi, ah, yuck!

PAUL (going to Mimi and taking her arm again)

I'm not gainsaying it!

MIMI (confused)

Ah! Sir—and I made you scrub my room!

(Estragon, goes over to Paul.)

PAUL (laughing and pointing to Seraphin)

Yes—but it's he who— (makes a scrubbing gesture)

MIMI

Really? (bursting into laughter) Him? Ah, ha, ha, ha!

SERAPHIN (laughing also)

Ah! Ah! Ah!

ESTRAGON

Huh? What? I don't get it. (aside) I'm going to tell Hortense!

CHORUS

Ah! Who wouldn't love a grisette,

Honest and flirtatious?

No, nothing is better hereabouts

Than youth, love, and fresh attractions.

CURTAIN

THE TYPE YOU DON'T MARRY
BY ÉDOUARD PAILLERON

CAST OF CHARACTERS

EUGENE SAVIGNAC

GEORGE MAUREL

ADRIENNE, George's Mistress

BERTHE, an old friend of Adrienne's

CONSTANCE, a chamber maid

THE PLAY

A small dining room.

EUGENE:

(entering) Is Mr. Maurel here yet?

CONSTANCE:

(locking a drawer in a desk at the right) Mr. George is with Madame. I think he's finishing a letter. (arranging flowers in vases on the table)

EUGENE:

Don't disturb yourself; I'm in no hurry. (sitting by the fire) I'm going to get warm. What are all those flowers for?

CONSTANCE:

(mysteriously) Why, sir, I cannot tell you, it's a secret. Ask the cat. (talking to the kitten) The cat replies, "It's a great big secret." Isn't that what you say, darling? (taking both vases with an air of triumph) I have to run to the market. So. Isn't it like Spring? Who would say it's the 20th of November?

EUGENE:

One more anniversary! You're always exposed to some celebration here.

CONSTANCE:

(coming closer and closer to Eugene) Everyone loves each other here, Mr. Eugene. Even the cat who loves us all and brings us luck. You should love us a little. Make an effort. Then they won't tremble when you come. And when there's a secret— Hush! They're coming.

GEORGE:

(letter in hand, entering) You came just as I was writing you. You should have come ten minutes earlier.

EUGENE:

(rising) Lazy boy! Do you have a cigar?

(Constance goes out. Eugene looks around to see if they are alone.)

EUGENE:

While we're alone, you haven't forgotten about tonight? At six-thirty.

GEORGE:

Well, sort of. I was going to explain to you. (handing him the letter) Or write you.

EUGENE:

(after reading it, tears it up) There!

GEORGE:

But my friend—

EUGENE:

Do you know why they want to keep you here? (looking at the desk drawer) It's in there for sure. I saw Constance locking it with a key. You cannot back out now. How will it look?

GEORGE:

I am counting on you to excuse me. Make up something.

EUGENE:

I'm not going to mix in this any further. Yes or no? Are you determined to marry this girl?

GEORGE:

Absolutely. (low) What I lack is courage.

EUGENE:

(laughing) Courage.

GEORGE:

We're constructed differently.— Do you think I can forget six happy years?

EUGENE:

(shrugging his shoulders) Come on. I'm listening to you.

GEORGE:

I can still see myself in the rue Picard one winter. Every day, I killed time until they went out.

EUGENE:

And you followed them through deserted streets until Adrienne was all alone. And when all her friends had gone, you accosted her. And she let you kiss her hand. (rising) And you've done nothing more ever since.

GEORGE:

(rising too) You have a different way of being in love. That friend of Adrienne's, that Bertha.

EUGENE:

(unable to remember, but trying) Bertha.

GEORGE:

The little brunette.

EUGENE:

Oh! She's ancient history. It's been five years—yes, I saw her yesterday all dressed up, but for the life of me, I couldn't put a name to that pretty face.

GEORGE:

You've never been in love. If you had, you'd know why I lack courage. Do you understand why I lack courage?

EUGENE:

Put it in a book or in verse. Don't become serious at your age.

GEORGE:

But I am very serious, I assure you.

EUGENE:

Let it go! Do you intend to live socially? You are not taking into account the falsity of your position. Your father, and not only your father, your aunt, your grandmother, all your family. Whenever I mention your name to them, they don't smile, they don't raise an eyebrow. Your father changes the subject whenever your name is mentioned. You've broken with your family. Separated from society. As for morality—

GEORGE:

(laughing) You don't know how funny some words sound in your mouth. (sitting) Morality!

EUGENE:

Yes, morality. And why, if you please, does it sound funny coming from me? I've lived and I've learned. It won't financially ruin you. But you are breaking all the rules. You are a living scandal. Marry your mistress: whoever heard of it!

GEORGE:

I should never have taken a mistress; but having taken one, as I took Adrienne, I will marry her.

EUGENE:

I'll end by worrying about you. But I will save you in spite of yourself. It's four now. I'm going to go home and change. Yes, or no? Are you coming?

GEORGE:

I'll see. I'd have to have an excuse.

EUGENE:

I bet Adrienne won't suspect anything. She's a woman, and if she has the least opportunity to please herself— If a friend were to visit her.

GEORGE:

She has no friends. She broke with everyone for me.

EUGENE:

I'll be looking for you. (leaving)

ADRIENNE:

(runs in very happy) Look. (bending to show him her hairdo) Isn't it me? You were right. It becomes me very much.

GEORGE:

It looks good on you. You have great taste.

ADRIENNE:

Tonight we're going to have a candlelight dinner together.

GEORGE:

(stammering) I—f-forgot to mention to you—

ADRIENNE:

What?

GEORGE:

(lowering his eyes) I promised—you know, to dine with my uncle.

ADRIENNE:

(indignant) No. Absolutely not. Tonight you are mine. I am keeping you.

GEORGE:

Don't get angry. Gene came, you heard him. I don't want to go. I know I promised you. But Gene says this dinner's very important—a lot of important people will be there. (trying to kiss Adrienne, who pushes him away angrily; he turns toward the door at the right)

ADRIENNE:

(following him) Where are you going?

GEORGE:

To put on my coat. Be reasonable. I've just got time. I'll come back to say goodbye. (trying to leave)

ADRIENNE:

(putting herself resolutely in front of the door) No, I'm keeping you.

GEORGE:

Heavens, you are going to get me into a fight with my uncle.

ADRIENNE:

Your uncle! Your cousin! As far as I'm concerned, these people do not exist.

GEORGE:

If I don't go, my future might—

ADRIENNE:

Your future? And me! And me! (bursting into tears, then sweetly) Don't you see how I'm suffering?

GEORGE:

(pulling her into his arms) My Adrienne.

ADRIENNE:

I don't know what you told me or what I said. I was only thinking of one thing. Can't you guess? You haven't suddenly forgotten?

GEORGE:

(trying to remember) Forgotten?

ADRIENNE:

(with a sad smile) Sir, what day is it today? Isn't it our—

GEORGE:

(remembering suddenly) Oh, pardon.

ADRIENNE:

(in a tone of self-reproach) You did forget! But, you wouldn't have. (going to the desk where the flowers are) Constance, who is only our servant, didn't forget.

GEORGE:

Forgive me.

ADRIENNE:

(softening) The 20th of November. (counting on her fingers) Six years. Time passes so fast.

GEORGE:

It seems like yesterday to me. It was snowing. You recall the snow that day? (they sit, George is on the footstool)

ADRIENNE:

Yes. I was cold.

GEORGE:

I lit a big fire.

ADRIENNE:

(dreamily) And if I hadn't—where would I be?

GEORGE:

(very choked up) Don't worry. I love you.

ADRIENNE:

Truly? A little still as before?

GEORGE:

(hugging her) A hundred times more. I've never loved you more. (shivering) Brr! It's cold. Let's light a big fire. I'll stay.

ADRIENNE:

(delighted, rising) You'll stay. (she rings)

CONSTANCE:

(entering) Yes, Madame!

ADRIENNE:

Bring his coat.

GEORGE:

(surprised) What?

ADRIENNE:

(smiling) I'm not a child. You remember, you love me. That's enough. We'll celebrate tomorrow.

GEORGE:

(very touched) How good you are!

(Constance returns with George's coat)

ADRIENNE:

(simply) Let me retie your tie. I want you to shine at your uncle's.

GEORGE:

No, I'd rather stay.

CONSTANCE:

Yes, sir. To the devil with everyone else. A day like today doesn't come often.

ADRIENNE:

Don't tempt me, George. Go quickly or I won't let you go. (a pause)

GEORGE:

You're worth more than I am. (Kisses her and leaves. Constance is furious and shows it as she removes the tablecloth and hurls it on the table.)

ADRIENNE:

(laughing) Well, I still intend to eat even though I'll be alone. (kindly) I know you planned something. Thanks. And tomorrow.

CONSTANCE:

(through her teeth) Tomorrow! Who knows about tomorrow?

(Adrienne goes to her room)

ADRIENNE:

(off) Tell me when dinner is ready.

CONSTANCE:

Nice anniversary! Oh, my poor flowers. (A bell rings. Constance, hoping that George has returned, rushes to the door and opens it. Then, disappointed.) Oh, Miss Bertha.

BERTHA:

Yes, it's me. Tell Adrienne, will you.

(Constance goes out. Bertha paces nervously. Then goes to Adrienne as she enters and kisses her.)

ADRIENNE:

(a bit coldly) Sit down.

BERTHA:

It's been a long time. A lot of water under the dam since we last met. You've become an honest woman. Very cozy here. (smelling the air) Very domestic. Positively. But, why are you looking at me so carefully? Is there something strange about me?

ADRIENNE:

It seems to me you used to be a brunette.

BERTHA:

(rising and laughing) Blondes have more fun. (looking in the mirror) Don't you think it goes well with me? Since I last saw you I've travelled a lot. Been to Monaco, Italy.

ADRIENNE:

(whose coldness has worn off) Still the same.

BERTHA:

I wrote you. Are you still happy?

ADRIENNE:

Still.

BERTHA:

George still loves you?

ADRIENNE:

Why, yes. Still.

BERTHA:

(in an odd tone) Oh!

ADRIENNE:

Does that surprise you?

BERTHA:

No. It's funny. Men are all the same. Come on.

ADRIENNE:

(starting to become nervous) Why do you say that?

BERTHA:

Oh, for no reason. Do you still see Eugene? I met him just now. I went with him to his home.

ADRIENNE:

(more and more uneasy) Why do you tell me all this? Of course we still see Mr. Savignac.

BERTHA:

(compassionately) Poor friend.

ADRIENNE:

Look! Out with it!

BERTHA:

Listen. I know what you want from me. But it's a service that one only does for a friend. I came right away. I'll tell you now. (they sit down)

ADRIENNE:

(very unnerved) What is it all about?

BERTHA:

My God. You know I'm very curious. I saw a letter at Eugene's and I read it.

ADRIENNE:

(anxiously) Well?

BERTHA:

Eugene gave me the details. George is marrying a young woman; very rich, of course.

ADRIENNE:

(protesting) No!

BERTHA:

Don't take it so hard. It happens to everybody. It's life.

ADRIENNE:

I cannot cry.

BERTHA:

Why should you cry? It's a hard moment to get through, but afterwards one is stronger for it. I've just rendered you a famous service.

ADRIENNE:

(hiding her face in her hands) Oh! I didn't know how to keep him.

CONSTANCE:

Shall I set the table?

ADRIENNE:

(to Bertha) What are you doing tonight? Nothing, right? (to Constance) Set two places.

BERTHA:

Oh, I cannot, darling. They must be waiting for me already. I'm dining at Maxim's. The place I wanted to take you that day George got so angry with me. Come soon. I invite you.

ADRIENNE:

Oh, no thanks.

BERTHA:

(laughing) Bah! You're afraid. They won't eat you. Come on. When you're in pain, you've got to drown it. I assure you, the dinners are very good and the company very gay.

ADRIENNE:

(with a shiver) Thanks. I don't want to go. (sitting down)

BERTHA:

What a baby! But, darling, you have to be strong. If I leave you, you're going to cry yourself to sleep. Put on your hat.

ADRIENNE:

No.

BERTHA:

As you wish. (going to the door) Bye now. I regret having told you. (returning) It seems she's a blonde. Eugene told me she's not as pretty as you. Not very tall, but nice to look at.

ADRIENNE:

Goodbye. Leave me alone, I beg you.

BERTHA:

It's just that it infuriates me to see you cry. Come on. I promise you George isn't crying. By now he's sitting beside her.

ADRIENNE:

(faintly echoing) Yes—beside her.

BERTHA:

Like two lovebirds. The way you once were.

ADRIENNE:

(weakly) Yes, yes. As we once were.

BERTHA:

Still, perhaps you are right to take this so quietly. Goodbye.

ADRIENNE:

(running after her) Come back. Let's go to my room. I'm going to get my hat.

CONSTANCE:

(alone, stupefied, troubled) Madame! Madame! It's impossible.

(After a pause Eugene enters with George.)

GEORGE:

(shrugging his shoulders) With Bertha, especially. I tell you, you didn't see what you think you did. (To Constance) Where's Adrienne?

CONSTANCE:

(embarrassed) Sir!

EUGENE:

You see!

GEORGE:

Where is she?

CONSTANCE:

She left with a lady.

GEORGE:

Will she be back for dinner? (silence) Did she say when she would be back? (silence) All right. Leave us. (Constance leaves) (agitated) Well? What do you say?

EUGENE:

(getting warm by the fire) Me? Nothing.

GEORGE:

What do you advise me to do?

EUGENE:

Me? Nothing. Why ask my advice? You wouldn't listen to me.

GEORGE:

(who hasn't listened to him) Could she possibly be with Bertha?

EUGENE:

After all, it's human enough. If you knew women, you wouldn't be angry with Adrienne. After six years, one night you dine in town, and the dear child goes out to distract herself with a gay girlfriend. You see, it's good for our sisters and mothers to wait for us at home, playing the piano.

GEORGE:

(still preoccupied) When I wanted to stay, she pushed me out the door. What's bad is not knowing. Yes, she's cheating on me.

EUGENE:

To cheat, to be cheated, that's life. Still, I confess it's less pleasant to be cheated on.

GEORGE:

Then, right away. I don't want to be a coward any longer.

EUGENE:

Spoken like a man. (shaking his hand)

GEORGE:

I never want to see her again. I'll write her and tell her everything is over.

CONSTANCE:

(entering) Madame has just returned.

GEORGE:

Alone?

CONSTANCE:

Alone.

GEORGE:

Where is she?

CONSTANCE:

In her room.

GEORGE:

What's she doing?

CONSTANCE:

She's locked herself in. I think she's crying.

EUGENE:

(seeing George heading for Adrienne's room) Where are you going?

GEORGE:

I want to see her.

EUGENE:

And your resolutions?

GEORGE:

Leave me alone.

EUGENE:

If you see her, you're ruined. She'll convince you of whatever she wants to. (George goes out) Whew! That was close (ringing, Constance returns) I want to speak to Madame.

(Constance leaves. Eugene twirls his hat in his hand. Adrienne appears.)

EUGENE:

Miss.

ADRIENNE:

Sir.

EUGENE:

I've been asked to tell you something.

ADRIENNE:

(hiding her emotions) I am listening to you, sir.

EUGENE:

You know how much I love George. He's like a younger brother to me.

ADRIENNE:

(falling into a chair) I beg your pardon. I need to sit down.

EUGENE:

Of course, of course. No ceremony with me. You must have been expecting this for a long time. Everything comes to an end. Youth passes. The serious age in life arrives. You have to conform to the demands of the world.

ADRIENNE:

(almost to herself) Is that what George had to tell me?

EUGENE:

George has been thinking about your future.

ADRIENNE:

(wounded) Oh!

EUGENE:

His dearest wish is that you should lack nothing. That you should be in an independent position.

ADRIENNE:

I thank him.

EUGENE:

And to make things easier he asked me to give you this. (putting a billfold on the table)

ADRIENNE:

(disgusted) That's all, isn't it?

EUGENE:

All! It goes without saying that whatever is here, furniture, jewels belongs to you. And if ever you are unhappy, George counts on your applying to him.

ADRIENNE:

(holding back her tears) Well. You've forgotten nothing. You do your work admirably. In my turn, I will ask you to do something for me. Wait for me. Watch my fortune. (she goes to her room)

EUGENE:

(alone) Going nicely. Very well done on all sides. Civilized.

BERTHA:

(entering) Where is she? Heavens, you here! Everything was going fine at first, but it all started to unravel. Anyway, I earned that bracelet you promised me. (calling) Adrienne! Adrienne! (to Eugene) You know George is downstairs.

EUGENE:

Shut up! She's coming.

(Adrienne enters, dressed for leaving, as George appears in the doorway at the left.)

ADRIENNE:

(not seeing George) You will tell George.

GEORGE:

(coming in rapidly) You are leaving?

ADRIENNE:

(noticing him) Ah, you're back. I prefer explaining this to you. Perhaps I would have said things to him—

GEORGE:

(softened to jelly) Yes, tell me. Tell me everything.

(They come forward)

ADRIENNE:

I no longer know what has happened to me. We were still so happy just a few hours ago. Well, perhaps it is for the best. Everything has to end.

GEORGE:

Listen—

ADRIENNE:

I don't want your money. I prefer to leave. I won't take anything. I'm leaving as I came—with nothing. Goodbye. (going to the door)

GEORGE:

(following her) Adrienne!

ADRIENNE:

No, let me go. That will be better. I understand I am in your way. Don't worry about me. I will go back to work. Goodbye.

GEORGE:

(grabbing her, holding her in his arms) Adrienne! My wife! (to Eugene) My wife! (low to Adrienne) I love you.

(Constance enters and joyously resets the table, placing a huge cake on the table.)

GEORGE:

That's it, Constance, Hurry up. I'm hungry as can be!

CONSTANCE:

(giving Eugene his billfold) This is yours, sir.

EUGENE:

(sighing, putting his billfold in his pocket) Well! Morality is defeated! (looking at his watch)

Come on, Bertha, I'll take you to dinner.

CURTAIN

MARRIED SINCE NOON
BY WILLIAM BUSNACH AND ARMAND LIORAT, MUSIC BY GEORGES JACOBI

CAST OF CHARACTERS

ESTELLE PARADICE

THE PLAY

A very small room. A window in cutaway. Doors at rear and on both sides. A cupboard set in the wall, and a chimney with a lit fire. Not far away from the fireplace, a sofa. A covered table with a lit lamp. A small desk. On the chimney a clock and candelabra. Not very luxurious but quite comfortable.

AT RISE, Estelle is alone in a wedding gown. Her back is to the audience.

ESTELLE:

(to her unseen mother) Come on, goodbye, my dear little mother.— No, I assure you I really prefer to undress by myself. Good night.

Come on, don't cry!

(she shuts the door and comes forward)

Mother didn't want to leave; she pretended that it is no longer customary for a mother to leave her daughter alone at such a solemn moment. She absolutely wanted to wait for me until Anatole—but as for me, I didn't want it. I need to gather my ideas. Because I'm not dreaming. Here I am in my husband's place. My husband! There's no more to say about it. This morning, when I got up, I was still Miss Simmoneau, and since noon, my name is Mrs. Anatole Paradice. It will soon be twelve hours ago. Twelve big hours. What a day, my God! I thought I would never see it end.

(sings)

Dressing up—starting at six

All weepy, Mama proceeds to put me in

In white from head to toe.

It seems it's a symbol.

Then a hired carriage

Comes to get me—and there we are

All four left for the church,

Mom and me, my fiancé and Papa.

During the Mass, Anatole

Placed a ring on my finger.

Indeed, that's another symbol.

I really don't know why—

Soon the ceremony

Passes to the sacristy.

Relatives, friends hang on my neck,

Especially my cousin Jules.

Who kissed me and hugged me a lot.

The wedding party

Gets back in the carriage.

Clip, clop.

We take a tour of the lake.

At the waterfall

We get out

And everyone in a file,

Passes under it. I do, too.

Is this yet another symbol?

What I know is—is that Anatole

Allowed himself in the darkness

To be a little too frisky.

For barely an hour

We strolled.

Then we left the Bois, and without further delay

The coachman drove us at a trot

To dine at the Lemaidelay.

We ate, drank, got very free

I participate in the frivolity.

But at dessert, I suddenly feel

That near my foot, a hand was sliding.

And I recognized it was my cousin.

"Jules, will you please shut up!"

How I screamed! Everyone laughed. "Calm down, will you."

They said it was a symbol.

The youngest bachelor always

Must detach the bride's garter.

And they divvy up the ribbons.

Then without wasting time

They rush

To start dancing.

My word; from embarrassment

I would, had it been possible,

Have counted all the arms

That pressed me.

That ruffled me.

Never had I been so embarrassed.

Still

Towards eleven o'clock, with a nasty air

I see them smiling, hushing up

Mama approaches and in a trembling tone

Says to me "Estelle, we're clearing out."

Blushing,

Happy, suspicious of things I'm ignorant of

I came into this room

Asking if there still remains

Some symbol to be shown me.

So here I am at his place, my place, in fact.

Because, after all, it's for the two of us that he rented this jewel of an apartment. Our nest, as he's been calling it for the last week, making naughty eyes at me. Why's he been making naughty eyes at me for the last week? The fact is, it's a bit funny. A nest on the third floor of Madame de Sentier! But here we are. Papa who never left the linen trade insisted absolutely that we remain in the neighborhood, and the house belongs to Mr. Dumont, the person who arranged our marriage. Mr. Anatole, in fact—I can actually call him simply Anatole—indeed, I need to begin calling him simply Anatole. Anatole is his grandson, and I think that if Mr. Dumont insisted on arranging this marriage, it was especially to rent out his second little apartment which had been vacant for three terms.

But that doesn't matter. I like him all the same, because— Between ourselves, I didn't want to place Saint Catherine's bonnet on this hair—and besides, he's a very fine man, this Mr. Dumont. With very austere manners from all appearances. I often heard Mama say when speaking of him, "He's a man of very austere manners." And Papa added, "A Joseph, what."

(considering)

His first name is Hamilcar. So why'd Papa call him Joseph? Doubtless that means a man who behaves very properly. I hope my husband is also a Joseph.

(looking at the clock)

Eleven thirty-five. And it's at midnight exactly that Anatole— Heavens! Here! Now, I'm almost used to it. That Anatole who remained at the restaurant to play cards with Papa—will come to find me. He ought to have wanted to come immediately. He was getting up when he saw me leaving, but Papa wouldn't have it.

"Not at all, not at all, sir," he said to him. "Estelle must enter the conjugal domicile under the wing of her mother. You will be informed."

Anatole sat back down quite pitifully. And right then Papa kissed me on my face. Oh, without emotion, that's him, not like my cousin Jules. Then he added. "Pay attention, young man. I see your game."

But time marches on. And he's going to come. God! How scared I am! Still, why should I be so afraid of this? He still doesn't have a nasty appearance, oh, no, to the contrary, but it's stronger than I am. It seems to me, I'll be less afraid tomorrow.— No, it's stupid to be afraid like this. It sends the blood to my head.

(She rids herself of her cloak and tosses it on a chair. A paper falls to the ground and she picks it up.)

Heavens! What's this? Ah, yes, the letter that I got this morning as I was getting in the carriage. I didn't even look at it. My head was really ready for that. Another prospectus probably. You cannot imagine how many prospectuses one receives when one is on the point of getting married. And lots of other amusing stuff. I kept them all so Anatole can explain them to me.

(looks at the signature)

My goodness! Why, it's Valentine's handwriting. Valentine, my best friend from school. Oh, how long it's been since we lost touch with each other. But, it's true; she's been married for two weeks, she, too—

(Confidentially)

And we actually promised each other once that the first to get married would to the other immediately. She's kept her promise.— Aw, that's sweet of her. Now here's a letter that arrived in the nick of time.

(she opens the letter excitedly)

(sings)

"My dear Estelle, although my time

May be very full, you conceive,

Still, I remain faithful

To the oath we took.

I want to tell you

Of my first step in my wife's role.

So it's done. Here I am a Madame.

Oh, it's quite simple, you will see.

The same day of marriage

My spouse and I, without fancy manners

Took the Choo-Choo train from Lyon

As is customary.

So as to have the biggest place

Jules had rented for the two of us,

A first-class wagon.

You can imagine how happy he was!

Alone with him what extreme trouble.

He cuddled close and with a coaxing air

He murmured:

'How I love you.'

Gently he took my hand

Trembling, I let him do it.

When an employee who wasn't very decent

Abruptly opened the door,

To ask us for our tickets.

Fontainbeau! The train stopped.

And as it wasn't very late.

Jules proposed a private talk.

An excursion to Franchard.

We leapt into a small carriage.

Whip, coachman! And with a single bound

We went like an arrow

Through a woods three kilometers long.

At Franch we got down

And there, like two lovers,

We followed the shady paths.

But now, night was coming on.

After a few details more,

That I pass over in silence

We returned to the Charriot d'Or.

God, what a room, hardly sealed.

White curtains, pierced with holes.

A wall with nasty wallpaper—colored rose

That couldn't have cost six cents!

For furniture, two vulgar chairs.

An old armchair in red damascene.

And some huge engravings,

Belisarius and Leonidas.

Well, my dear, strange thing!

If I live to be a hundred

This little red room

No, I'll never forget it.

Ah! My Estelle— It would take me a long while

To tell you—but it suffices

You, you who are still a girl

And already I've told you too much.

Goodbye. Perhaps you're pissed at me.

You'll be married like me.

If I interrupt my letter at this point.

Your husband will tell you why."

(disappointed)

That's all. Well, I've really come

A long way. Ah, these married women!

Are they secretive! After that—

(looking at the clock again)

Twenty to twelve!

(crumpling the letter and looking around her)

It's nice here, and besides a short distance to the boulevard.

(going to the window and slightly raising the curtain)

Right across from my new acquaintance, Madame Pinson, who's married to my husband's friend—he's a tax collector. Oh, he's got very fine acquaintances, my husband. It's not surprising he's deputy chief of his office in the ministry, and I've been assured that once married, it will be very easy to get him decorated. It seems the Pinson household's very nice, and Papa said the other day, "They are not finches, they are turtledoves." Maybe we too, we'll be turtledoves. Here's our nest, Anatole said. A pretty little nest indeed. Just now as I came in I saw it; I was weeping in Mama's arms, but I saw it all the same. A small antechamber in a very fine style.

(looking)

What's that over there?

(opening a door)

Oh, it's the dining room.

(looking)

And over here? Ah, it's the—room.—

(she wanders around dreamily, then leaning on the chimney, she looks in the mirror.)

My poor crown! I actually think it's time to take it off.

(slowly she unhooks her crown and bouquet)

(sing)

Since it has to be, little flower

Depart my hair and my dress.

But don't worry.

Very soon you will be framed.

With regret, I see you fall

From my headdress.

It seems this adornment cannot last a single day.

Come on, so much the worse. Contrary to custom

I do not intend to rebel

It's a shame.

It's a shame

My poor orange flower.

Very soon it's apparent

Which flower goes well with me.

Bizarre thing! One day more

And it's no longer of any value.

How marvellously it went

With my corsage. And then suddenly—

It's strange! Why the dawn.

And why not the next day?

Come on, so much the worse, etc.

(speaking)

Meanwhile, I'm going to stroke it, quietly to put it in the shade of dust

(she places it on the table.)

Let's see, where am I going to put it? How annoying it is when one doesn't know the beings. Luckily, Anatole will show them to me.

(going to cupboard)

Ah, there it is exactly.

(opens it)

An armoire. My husband's wardrobe, and the washerwoman's basket.

(pulls out a small basket covered with a towel.)

It's not even used. How careless bachelors are. Men's linen. At home, I used to keep Papa's underwear straight. But it seems to me this ought not to be the same thing. Let's have a quick look.

(stopping)

What's always pleased me most about Anatole is that he always has very nice underwear.

(she pulls a lace dressing gown out of the basket and unfolds it.)

Huh! What's this one? This belongs to my husband? He wears lace at twelve francs a meter?

(looking quickly at the monogram)

B.A.

(she thinks about it.)

Those aren't his initials. What's this mean? Could it belong to a woman, by chance? Why, my husband has been living here for the last six weeks. A woman would then have come here before me!!! What to do? She might have left her dressing gown. Who could this woman be? He has no close relatives—and then besides!!! Why, in that case she'd be a villainous woman? O my God! And perhaps these infamies lasted a long while.

(taking the laundress' book and reading)

"August 26 Four handkerchiefs of fine cambric; 19th. two bonnets. 12th a chemise; 5th—three shorts."

(with a scream)

Why, it cannot be possible. Let's see— Anatole who seems so sweet—he's actually a— Ah, I really don't know what to call him.

Ah, how annoyed I am to have sent Mama away. She's been married a lot longer than I have. She must have had experiences like this. Let's see, let's not lose our head. Evidently, anyone who washes her linen in my husband's home must have left other traces of her passage here.

On this table, nothing. In this cupboard, a suit, a coat, a housecoat, a vest, two vests in all. All that is perfectly normal. Ah, a pair of pants.

(takes it out)

I've often heard it said there are women who wear the pants, but we won't speak of the pants.

(she throws them back in the armoire.)

Let's look elsewhere. In this chest of drawers.

(opening it)

Drawers.

(pulling out objects and naming them one by one.)

A pipe. A pair of gloves, size eight and a half. That's Anatole's size.

(opening more drawers)

Nothing in this.

(a third)

Ah!

(she removes and opens a small box and pulls a medallion from it suspended by a black velour)

I think this time it's significant. With hair in it. Anatole's hair— What infamy.

(she hurls the medallion to the floor)

This is frightful! He's a wretch! Ah, ah, Mama! Mama! My nerves!

(she falls onto a sofa in prey to a violent nervous crisis. Then abruptly she stops and seems to consider; she stands up, goes to bolt the door, then comes back, and goes to the sofa and resumes her nervous attack.)

Ah, help! I'm dying! I want to go away! I no longer want to be Mrs. Paradice. Mama! Mama!!

(suddenly stops again)

Let's be calm, strong, and dignified.

(looking at clock)

Quarter to twelve. I've got just time enough to abandon this domicile, besmirched by such shocking orgies! I shall leave it as I entered, without my conscience reproaching me for anything. I am going to return home. I will tell Papa—as long as he hasn't lost at cards. I will say to him:

"Daddy, the husband you chose for me is a monster! I've left him. Give me another one."

Yes, yes—that's the thing. We're leaving.

(She puts her cloak back on)

And when I think that just now, at the Bois de Boulogne, passing beneath the waterfall, he swore he never loved anyone except me.— I intend for him to know that I am no longer his dupe. I am going to write to him. Where is there some ink? Paper—pen? My God! It's infuriating not to know about things. But it will not be Anatole who teaches me them. Ah, in this book with my pencil from my dance notebook.

(writing)

"Sir—don't count on me anymore. My decision is definitive. You can recall to your side the creature whose linen dishonors your domicile at the same time it reveals the dishonesty of your feelings. I have the honor to be Estelle Simmoneau, formerly Mrs. Paradise."

There! Let's put it in plain sight. On the convicting evidence.

(she puts the notebook on the nightgown which has remained on the sofa)

I can dispense with putting the address. The name is on the cover.

(reading)

"The laundry list that belongs to you."

(picking it up and reading with astonishment)

"To Mr. Amilcar Dumont."

Ah, indeed! It's not Anatole's. It belongs to Joseph. Well, thanks. He receives fine nightgowns, the gentleman with pure morals! But what's going on? I have it. The laundress was mistaken as to the floor. In that case, Anatole is actually innocent.

Isn't it funny how quick I am to call him simply Anatole?

Wait a minute! Wait a minute! What about the medallion?

(picks it up and examines it attentively).

"To my little Estelle, in memory of September 18th." How can it be September 18th; today's only the 17th.

(looking at the clock)

Ah, it soon will be the 18th. He must probably be counting on my hanging on his neck in the morning. Let's leave him that little pleasure. Let's pretend to have seen nothing.

(she places the medallion in its box and the box in the drawer.)

Is it ridiculous to think like that! How simple it all was. And when I think that this nightgown would have caused—! Wait! Wait!

I am going to straighten up his laundry. Back to Joseph. He'll find it tomorrow morning. My, My!

(she opens the window and shuts it after having thrown out the basket. Then she raises the window curtain)

Good heavens. There's some light opposite at the Pinsons'. They are coming back from the ball. Our ball!

(waving to the other house)

(Sings)

Evening neighbor, evening neighbor.

(turning towards the audience)

No. They are chatting in a corner by the fire.

(looking again)

The lady's removing her hood.

Heavens! The gentleman's coming closer.

He's taking her hand. How he loves her!

All the same. Ah, how nice it is

To have a household of turtledoves.

On the other side of the courtyard.

My goodness! Around her supple waist

Look how he passes his arm!

How charming they are! The jolly couple.

So gently intertwined.

Like you see in pictures.

All the same, how nice it is.

To have a household of turtledoves.

I no longer can see what's going on.

Will they cease to be in agreement?

Not at all! See how he kisses her.

He's hugging her very tight!

Oh! It's a very bad thing

Not to have curtains.

(uttering a scream of surprise and then smiling)

All the same, how nice it is.

To have a household of turtledoves.

(rapping at the door)

Ah, my God! It's him! It's Anatole.

(looking at the clock)

Why, it's only five to midnight.

(very naively)

Perhaps his watch is fast.

(heads toward the door she bolted.)

CURTAIN

ABOUT THE AUTHOR

Frank J. Morlock has written and translated many plays since retiring from the legal profession in 1992. His translations have also appeared on Project Gutenberg, the Alexandre Dumas Père web page, Literature in the Age of Napoléon, Infinite Artistries.com, and Munsey's (formerly Blackmask). In 2006 he received an award from the North American Jules Verne Society for his translations of Verne's plays. He lives and works in México.

www.ingramcontent.com/pod-product-compliance
Lightning Source LLC
LaVergne TN
LVHW041620070426
835507LV00008B/349